YOU
KNOW
YOU'RE
FROM
CHCH WHEN...

To the wonderful people of Christchurch and Canterbury
and to the thousands of contributors to the YKYFCW Facebook page

At 12.51 p.m. on Tuesday, 22 February 2011, Christchurch was hit by a 6.3 magnitude earthquake.

Although technically an aftershock to the 7.1 magnitude earthquake of 4 September 2010, this shock's epicentre was closer and shallower, and so the devastation was unimaginably more catastrophic. With the CBD in ruins, suburbs and outlying areas destroyed, and with a sickening loss of life and injury, a grieving Canterbury was once again brought to its knees. The human, spiritual and financial costs were so much greater this time — the city, the region, and the nation were left reeling.

Could Cantabrians pick themselves up again for a second, far more serious, time? Absolutely. But with the gargantuan scale of the tasks ahead, and the uncertainty of the ongoing aftershocks, it was a big ask.

With limited clothing, food and shelter, no power, sewerage, water or phones … showers became a thing of the past, toilets sprung up outdoors, and barbecues were dusted off and brought neighbours together.

Step up the true red-and-black Cantab spirit …

In this spirit, dyed-in-the-wool Cantabrian Bruce Raines set up the 'You know you're from Christchurch when' Facebook page, which became an instant sensation and a lifeline for many of those affected by the earthquake. Postings flooded in from around the region and the world in their thousands, as, in their darkest moments and times of adversity, Cantabrians began to rebuild their community giggle by giggle …

You know you're from Christchurch when …, the book, shows you the other side of the coin from what the media has been showing. These highlights of a community 'making the best of' are brought to you as a fundraiser for the Christchurch Earthquake Mayoralty Fund.

Before you fly out of Christchurch, the pilot announces, 'Expect severe turbulence — should ease once we're off the ground.'

You tell your kids Santa will land on the lawn where the chimney is.

YOU KNOW YOU'RE FROM CHCH WHEN...

YOU KNOW YOU'RE FROM CHCH WHEN...

You start a BBQ-cleaning business
and retire three months later
as a millionaire.

You poke your own eye teaching yourself sign language for 'one-eyed'.

You stop using the term
'built like a brick sh*t-house'.

A 'splash-back' is not that nice thing on the wall behind your stove top.

YOU
KNOW
**YOU'RE
FROM
CHCH**WHEN...

YOU KNOW YOU'RE FROM CHCH WHEN...

You try to convince the guy or gal
you like to shower with you
to save water.

You tell people you love them ...
and you ain't even drunk.

YOU
KNOW
YOU'RE
FROM
CHCH WHEN...

You can laugh at the lowered 'boy-racers' as you hoooooon past them at 30km over the bumps in your car, 4WD ... or pushbike!

Suddenly you don't mind 'door-knockers', as most bring gifts now.

YOU KNOW YOU'RE FROM CHCH WHEN...

A bucket of sh*t is no longer
that old car you drive.

You sleep in one suburb, shower in another, collect water from another, and go to the toilet where you can.

And still smile and greet people like you are all one big family.

YOU KNOW YOU'RE FROM CHCH WHEN...

'Liquefaction' becomes slang:
'That guy is full of liquefaction.'
'I had some bad takeaways last night which
gave me a bad dose of liquefaction.'

And you change the words
to the Rolling Stones' song
'I can't get no ...'

You see a lovely park in another city and think it would make a good evacuation point.

YOU KNOW YOU'RE FROM CHCH WHEN...

YOU KNOW YOU'RE FROM CHCH WHEN...

If you are doing 30km,
you've got up to a good speed.

Your husband is now 'working from home' — which translates to 'sleeping in and watching sports'.

YOU KNOW YOU'RE FROM CHCH WHEN...

YOU KNOW YOU'RE FROM CHCH WHEN...

After another aftershock hits,
the family take guesses at
magnitude and location.

The only items you have on your shelves are the things you want to claim insurance on.

YOU KNOW YOU'RE FROM CHCH WHEN...

YOU KNOW YOU'RE FROM CHCH WHEN...

Your choice of clothes in the morning
is determined by sniffing them.

You forget the toilet paper,
and start looking at the garden plants.

YOU
KNOW
YOU'RE
FROM
CHCH WHEN...

YOU KNOW YOU'RE FROM CHCH WHEN...

Water is just as exciting as beer.

You hold a military-style briefing with your partner as to where you will both be throughout the day.

YOU KNOW YOU'RE FROM CHCH WHEN...

YOU KNOW YOU'RE FROM CHCH WHEN...

Meals on Wheels is delivered
by chopper.

You are all starting to look like honorary Bogans.

YOU KNOW YOU'RE FROM CHCH WHEN...

Your local drunk staggers,
when sober.

You have a roaring party, the place gets totally trashed, and you tell the landlord it was the 'aftershocks'.

YOU KNOW YOU'RE FROM CHCH WHEN...

You finally have a valid reason for wearing your girlfriend's knickers.

A 'self-cleaning toilet' is
a bucket upside down on
your garden sprinkler.

YOU
KNOW
YOU'RE
FROM
CHCH WHEN...

YOU KNOW YOU'RE FROM CHCH WHEN.

Your en suite has a vege garden,
a dog kennel and grass.

A catch-22 is ...
that the closest and only takeaway
is curry... and the closest and only
toilet is in your backyard garden.

YOU KNOW YOU'RE FROM CHCH WHEN...

YOU KNOW YOU'RE FROM CHCH WHEN...

You don't blame your local council for bad roads, paths or drainage.

A house having great indoor–outdoor
flow isn't a good thing.

YOU KNOW
YOU'RE NOW
FROM
CHCH WHEN...

School-leavers decide that a student loan on an $8,000 polytech carpentry course will end up making them more money than spending $35,000 to be a lawyer through uni.

You accidentally leave your car unlocked overnight on the street and the only thing taken is your water supply.

YOU KNOW YOU'RE FROM CHCH WHEN...

You hear that your car has been
towed from the central city and
it makes your day.

It takes a natural disaster for the traffic to be as bad as it is every day in Auckland.

YOU KNOW YOU'RE FROM CHCH WHEN...

It's perfectly normal at morning tea to talk about how much sleep you got last night, and everyone cheers when someone says they slept right through.

Sweeping your lawn is the norm when affected by liquefaction.

YOU'RE KNOW FROM CHCH WHEN...

The idea of drinking straight tap-water scares you more than earthquakes.

The council has bright and shiny new signs saying *Crack repair*.

YOU KNOW YOU'RE FROM CHCH WHEN...

Your kids stop asking
for a sandpit.

Going to the next home-game involves
a three-grand airfare.

YOU'RE KNOW FROM WHEN...

OH HOH

Saying 'nice crack' is referring to the roads rather than ...

Your niece in West London can walk
from her house to a Crusaders game,
but you can't.

YOU KNOW YOU'RE FROM CHCHCH WHEN...

The saying 'safe as houses' means nothing.

The main sports stadium is sponsored by an insurance company and the turf isn't insured.

YOU'RE KNOW FROM WHEN...

YOU KNOW YOU'RE FROM HOHO WHEN...

You finally get to experience an out-of-towner running for the door during a 5.1 while you and your friends just sit there watching him.

30 is the new speed limit
— as 50 gets you airborne.

YOU'RE KNOW FROM WHEN...

YOU KNOW YOU'RE FROM OHIO WHEN...

You miss the live media briefings
twice a day, and Jeremy and Evelyn.

You are no longer surprised by empty supermarket shelves, and spend time instead looking at the interesting stains/marks on the floors, trying to work out which products made them.

YOU KNOW YOU'RE FROM CHÖÖHÖH WHEN...

You have just realized what the 'new' smell is — chlorine in the water!

4WD owners finally get to use their vehicles for the purpose for which they were designed ...

YOU KNOW YOU'RE FROM CHCH WHEN...

YOU KNOW YOU'RE FROM CHCH WHEN...

Your cellphone vibrates and you jump under a table.

You go away to Wellington for the weekend and you see less sand at Petone beach than you do at home in the suburbs.

YOU KNOW YOU'RE FROM CHCH WHEN...

Owning a flash car with sports suspension is not a good thing.

There seems to be a lot of bricks for sale on Trade Me and the 'Buy, Sell and Exchange' — and each purchase comes with a free trailer of sand.

YOU'RE FROM CHCH WHEN...

YO YOU'RE R KNOW U'FRO M
CHCH WHEN...

You think you should have owned
a wheel-alignment company.

'Our house ... in the middle of our street'
is no longer just a line from a song.

YOU KNOW YOU'RE FROM CHCH WHEN...

YOU KNOW YOU'RE FROM CHCH WHEN...

You donate to the Red Cross
even though you've applied for
a hardship grant from them.

You have to shake the dust off your clothes before you bring your dry washing in.

YOU KNOW YOU'RE FROM CHCH WHEN...

You move cities, and every time you say the word 'Christchurch' everyone stops and listens.

The city's golf courses have extra hazards, and even Tiger's caddy can't advise on the best club for getting out of these.

YO YOU R E K N O W
U'FRO M
CHCH WHEN...

Half the children come from
'broken homes'.

Your children are excited
to be back at school instead
of complaining about it.

YO YOU DO R KNOW U'FRO E OM W
CHCH WHEN...

Your mum gets excited about a
different-coloured port-a-loo on
the side of the street.

You take your dirty washing
on holiday with you.

YOU'RE FROM CHCH WHEN...

YOU'RE KNOW YOU'RE FROM CHCH WHEN...

Digging a hole and pooping in your garden is no longer weird.

Your three-year-old points out the window
and says 'That building is buggered',
as you drive down the road.

YO YOU'RE KNOW FROM CHCH WHEN...

Your mayor has to explain
to Prince William what
'munted' means.

Your kitchen cupboards have bungy cords holding them closed to stop things falling out during aftershocks.

YOU KNOW YOU'RE FROM CHCH WHEN...

YOU KNOW YOU'RE FROM CHCH WHEN...

You see roadwork signs like
Temporary and *Work ends*
and you say 'Yeah right.'

Your city has so many men in uniform you think you must be in a Village People video.

YOU'RE FROM CHCH WHEN...

YOU'RE FROM CHCH WHEN... YOU KNOW YOU

Your brand-new, totally awesome
road bike finally arrived ...
and you instantly regret it isn't
a cheap mountain bike.

A For Sale sign reads:
This sand comes with a house.

YOU'RE KNOW YOU'RE FROM CHCH WHEN...

You have to share your new office space with two cats and a flatmate.

You go away on holiday and start getting homesick when you see army trucks and helicopters.

YOU'RE FROM CHCH WHEN... YOU KNOW YOU'RE

YOU KNOW YO U'RE FROM CHCH WHEN...

Being on holiday and drinking is
now known as liquard vacation.

You pause to consider whether
port-a-loos might attract lightning.

YOU'RE FROM CHCH WHEN... YOU KNOW

There's a big (ish) shake in the night and you say to your cat 'Don't move', and she purrs back to you.

The dog beats you to the doorframe.

YO U'RE FROM CHCH WHEN...

You go out on a Friday night and do the long, drunk walk home, and you have the pick of the toilets on the way.

You have to home-cook
your own junk food.

YOU'RE **NOW** **FR**O**M** CHCH **WHEN**...

Your power bill estimate is $600,
but you've had power for only
three days of the month.

You've had enough days without electricity already, so you plan to celebrate Earth Hour by turning your lights on.

YOU KNOW YOU'RE FROM CHCH WHEN...

YOU'RE FROM CHCH WHEN... YOU KNOW...

Going to Wellington to escape
earthquakes makes sense.

You have to sanitize your hands
after washing them.

YOU'RE FROM CHCH WHEN... YOU KNOW...

You're happy to be constipated.

Even guys know who
'Hot Jeremy' is.

YOU KNOW
YOU'RE NOW
FROM
CHCH WHEN...

Your budgie's new saying is
'It's munted ... it's munted ...
it's munted ...'

You realize you have an inbuilt seismograph you've never had to use before, and which is accurate to 0.5 magnitude.

YO K N
YOU'RE O
FROM W
CHCH WHEN...

A girl asks a guy if he's wearing
protection and he immediately thinks
about hard hats, hi-viz jackets
and elbow pads.

Your GPS overheats with all
the recalculating it has to do with
the route you take.

YOU KNOW YOU'RE FROM CHCH **WHEN...**

Even a radio DJ announces
he has quake belly.

You get your car back out of the CBD cordon and wonder 'Does my insurance cover the removal of USAR tagging?'

YOU KNOW YOU'RE FROM CHCH WHEN...

DO YOU
KNOW
YOU'RE
FROM
CHCH WHEN...

It is faster to get to work from Ashburton than from your house in Wainoni.

You can charge more for your rental property when there is a port-a-loo outside.

YOU KNOW YOU'RE FROM CHCH WHEN...

Instead of fantasizing about getting into someone else's pants, your biggest fantasy now is getting into a clean pair of your own!

You go all air-hostess with visitors: before serving them coffee, you hand them a safety card and advise of the nearest emergency exit.

YOU KNOW YOU'RE FROM CHCH WHEN...

YOU KNOW YOU'RE FROM CHCH WHEN...

You choose to do your
'retail therapy' online.

Your mum lets you get away with the mess in your room because it was 'the earthquake' that did it.

YOU KNOW YOU'RE FROM CHCH WHEN...

YOU KNOW YOU'RE FROM CHCH **WHEN...**

'Working from home' is no longer a euphemism for having a day off.

You are desperate for the plumber
to arrive, because the long drop
is becoming a short drop.

YOU KNOW YOU'RE FROM CHCH WHEN...

A blue box has landed outside your house and you don't think the Doctor has arrived in his Tardis.

You go *pfffff* when Wellington
has a 4.5 earthquake that's
40 kilometres deep.

YOU
KNOW
YOU'RE
FROM
CHCH WHEN...

YOU KNOW **YOU'RE FROM CHCH** WHEN...

Every house is a crack house.

Voluntarily staying in Timaru for five days seems like a good idea.

YOU KNOW YOU'RE FROM CHCH WHEN...

YOU KNOW YOU'RE FROM CHCH WHEN...

The answer to everything is
'It's on the floor.'

You have been teaching yourself sign language, as you now know how important it is. But so far, without realizing it, you have: told a cop to piss off, married four people while stuck in rush-hour traffic, told your mate's grandmother you want to be more than friends, and again poked yourself in the eye trying to sign 'one-eyed Cantabrian'.

YOU
KNOW
YOU'RE
FROM
CHCH WHEN...

YOU KNOW YOU'RE FROM CHCH WHEN...

City humidity is up 80% due to boiling water.

'Open home' takes on a
whole new meaning.

YOU
KNOW
YOU'RE
FROM
CHCH WHEN...

YOU KNOW YOU'RE FROM CHCH WHEN...

Even a stomach rumble scares you.

Hi-viz is the new black.

YOU KNOW YOU'RE FROM **CHCH** WHEN…

YOU KNOW YOU'RE FROM CHCH WHEN...

You start talking back
to the aftershocks.

Your mother uses the word 'munted' in casual conversation.

YOU
KNOW
**YOU'RE
FROM
CHCH**WHEN…

This book has been designed and typeset by a Canterbury-based business. A percentage of the proceeds of this book will be donated to the Christchurch Earthquake Mayoralty Fund .

HarperCollins *Publishers*

First published 2011
HarperCollinsPublishers (New Zealand) Limited
P.O. Box 1, Auckland 1140

HarperCollins *Publishers*
31 View Road, Glenfield, Auckland 0627, New Zealand
25 Ryde Road, Pymble, Sydney, NSW 2073, Australia
A 53, Sector 57, Noida, UP, India
77–85 Fulham Palace Road, London W6 8JB, United Kingdom
2 Bloor Street East, 20th Floor, Toronto, Ontario M4W 1A8, Canada
10 East 53rd Street, New York, NY 10022, USA

National Library of New Zealand Cataloguing-in-Publication Data
You know you're from Christchurch when-- / compiled by Bruce Raines.
ISBN 978-1-86950-946-0
1. Earthquakes—Social aspects—New Zealand—Christchurch—Humor.
2. Canterbury Earthquake, N.Z., 2010—Humor. 3. New Zealand wit and humor. 4. Christchurch (N.Z.)—Social life and customs—Humor.
I. Raines, Bruce. II. Title.
363.3495099383—dc 22

ISBN: 978 1 86950 946 0
Cover design and typesetting by Book Design Ltd. www.bookdesign.co.nz
Printed by Printlink Wellington